Invisible Scars

Healing the Adult Child of Narcissistic Parents

DR. THOMAS JUBY

BlueRose ONE.com
Stories Matter
NewDelhi • London

BLUEROSE PUBLISHERS
India | U.K.

For permissions requests or inquiries regarding this publication, please contact:

BLUEROSE PUBLISHERS
www.BlueRoseONE.com
info@bluerosepublishers.com
+91 8882 898 898
+4407342408967

ISBN: 978-93-7310-932-9

Cover design: Aafiya Saifi
Typesetting: Manisha Rawat

First Edition: January 2026

Preface

A Survivor's Voice

I wrote this book as someone who has survived the unpredictable and often unseen storms caused by a narcissistic parent. I know what it feels like to carry invisible wounds, with scars in the mind, heart, and even the body. For decades, I believed my feelings were wrong, my needs were selfish, and my very existence depended on pleasing someone who could never truly love me. I learned to shrink, disappear, and become whatever was needed to survive. Surviving, however, is not the same as living. I only realized the difference much later in life. For me, survival and living were one and the same, with no distinction between the two.

Every child deserves unconditional love, care, security, and provision. Unfortunately, some of us did not receive this warmth from our parents or our primary care givers. This absence left us hollow inside. This book is for any adult child who still feels the burden of conditional love, the guilt of saying no, and the confusion over their identity. It is for those who want to recover their life, identity, and happiness—not by changing the narcissist, but by changing their own behavior and reactions to the past. Remember, you might feel broken, but I see you as a survivor who refuses to stay small. Much love, dear readers. And ye shall know the truth, and the truth shall make you free. John 8:32 KJV

Introduction
Reclaiming Your Life

If you're reading this book, chances are you've spent a lot of your life attempting to navigate the complexities, with a million questions raging through your head. You may have grown up questioning your worth, doubting your feelings, and feeling a constant pressure to perform, appease, or disappear. Perhaps you've struggled with relationships, boundaries, or even knowing who you truly are outside of the shadow of parental control. You are not alone. Millions of adult children of Narcissistic parents share this experience. The challenges are real, deep, and often invisible to those who haven't lived them. When I left my home for college, I thought all chaos was over, and I was free. However, the patterns of self-doubt, over-responsibility, perfectionism, and emotional hyper-vigilance persisted well into my adulthood. Which surely affected my career choices, romantic relationships, friendships, and above all, my relationship with myself. I struggled with self-image, worth, and value.

The focus of this book is to heal and not to blame. Blaming in such situation is easy and natural response. But it will not allow us to heal and will keep our focus on the other person's actions. It will rob us of our opportunity to heal. I truly believe that they who hurt us may also not have received unconditional love or care. It's only hurting people who hurt others. The only way to beat darkness is by shedding light. The only way to break the illusions is by the truth. We overcome evil with good. Be not overcome by evil, but overcome evil with good. Romans 12:21 KJV.

Take your time to forgive them and release them. By the end of the day, it's about your freedom, growth, and empowerment. Let me remind you, healing is not linear, and some days will feel heavier than others. But every step you take, no matter how small, is a step toward reclaiming the life you were always meant to live. Your experiences are valid. Your feelings matter. And most importantly, you are not broken — you were adapting. Now it is your time to thrive.

A bold and loving reminder - Healing from the impact of narcissistic parenting is not linear. There will be setbacks, difficult emotions, and moments of doubt. Yet each act of self-compassion, each boundary you enforce, each step you take toward reclaiming your identity is a victory. My aim through this book is to help you transform from survival mode into thriving mode. Again, I remind you that your feelings are valid, your needs are legitimate, and your life is yours to shape. You are not broken. You are not defined by what you endured. You are capable of love, joy, authenticity, and freedom. You are a wonderful human.

Contents

Contents

Chapter 1: Breaking The Illusion

"It wasn't love. It was control dressed up as care."

There comes a moment — quiet but unmistakable — when you realize that the story you were told about your childhood doesn't quite fit the feelings that live in your body.

It might happen while listening to a friend talk about her mother's warmth and encouragement, and something inside you goes still. Or perhaps you find yourself scrolling through articles late at night, typing words you never thought could apply to your family: *narcissistic parent.*

That's when it begins — the unraveling.

You start to see that what you once thought was love was often manipulation, that what you believed was "normal" was actually emotional neglect. You begin to understand that you weren't "too sensitive," you were simply never allowed to feel safe.

"It wasn't love. It was control dressed up as care."

The Silent Contract

Growing up with a narcissistic parent often means living under an unspoken contract:

"You exist to make me feel good about myself."

As children, we sign it without knowing. We become what they need — the helper, the achiever, the peacemaker, the invisible one — anything that keeps the peace and earns a scrap of affection. We are their extension.

Our lives revolve around anticipating moods, avoiding conflict, and performing just enough to stay on the "good" side. But the cost is immense.

Somewhere along the way, you lose yourself. The concept of Self vanishes with or without your knowledge. You slowly become their shadow as a child. Your authentic self-diminishes. You learn that your worth depends on others' approval. You measure your value by how well you serve, how little you need, how much you please.

And when love feels conditional for so long, self-love becomes foreign — almost suspicious. The concept of self-love becomes sin.

The Hidden Wounds

The wounds of growing up with a narcissistic parent are often invisible. There are no bruises, no broken bones — just a deep, quiet ache that whispers, *"Something's wrong with me."*

You might struggle with chronic self-doubt.

You might find yourself apologizing for existing, overexplaining, shrinking so others can shine.

You might stay in relationships that feel familiar — the same cycles of giving, fixing, and yearning for love that never quite arrive.

And yet, even with all the confusion and pain, there's a brilliance in survivors.

Because you had to read people so carefully, you developed a deep empathy.

Because you lived in emotional chaos, you developed a fierce intuition.

Because you were denied love, you learned to crave truth.

This book honors that resilience — not to romanticize the pain, but to show you that your sensitivity, your insight, your hunger for real connection are not weaknesses.

They are signs of your spirit refusing to be erased.

Breaking the Spell

When we grow up in narcissistic families, the illusion is strong.

We are told we are lucky. We are told our parents “Sacrificed everything.”

We are told we are ungrateful when we question, selfish when we assert, dramatic when we hurt.

The narcissistic family survives by twisting perception — by making the child doubt their own reality. So, the first step of healing isn’t forgiveness, or even detachment, it’s in your ability to see the truth and accepting it. The TRUTH SHALL SET YOU FREE. "And ye shall know the truth and the truth shall make you free" (KJV) John 8:32

To say:

Yes, they hurt me.

Yes, my needs were ignored.

Yes, I deserved better.

This is not about blaming or labeling for revenge. It’s about naming what happened so you can finally step out of the fog. You cannot heal from a story you’re still denying. I know how lonely this road can feel. For years, I was in denial. For years, I thought something was wrong with me. I thought if I could just be more patient, more forgiving, less reactive they would finally see me, love me, soften.

But narcissistic parents don’t see their children as separate people only as reflections of their own needs. This book I believe, is both psychological and personal a map and a mirror. I invite you to reflect, to write, to feel — gently, safely. I hope you will learn to mother or father your own inner child the one who has waited so long to be seen. When I finally understood that, something inside me broke open. Grief, anger, confusion, and relief poured out together.

It was the death of an illusion and the birth of freedom. Freedom comes with a price. Growth comes with a price. Freedom is not free. Growth is twinned with pain. Journey was not easy, but today I can say it's worth it. I'm happy to finally meet myself. So, as you move through these pages, take your time. Pause when it hurts. Rest when you need to. Remind yourself it's a healing pain.

This book isn't just about understanding them it's about understanding you. Because you were buried under years of conditioning, guilt, and survival. And every time you choose truth, you choose life. I truly want you to enjoy the freedom.

Chapter 2:
The Narcissistic Parent Blueprint

"They made you the mirror — and called it love."

Understanding Narcissism Beyond the Label

"Narcissism" has become one of the most overused and misunderstood words of our time.

It's easy to imagine it as vanity — someone obsessed with their reflection or desperate for attention. But in reality, pathological narcissism runs far deeper. It's not simply self-love; it's *the absence* of genuine self-worth[1][2]. A narcissistic parent doesn't truly see themselves as good or whole. They carry a hidden void — an unhealed wound from their own childhood, often buried under layers of grandiosity, control, and denial. They project confidence and authority, but inside, there's an emptiness that must constantly be filled by others' admiration, compliance, or pain. Their children become the mirrors that reflect back the parents' desired image — obedient, grateful, exceptional, or broken enough to make the parent feel powerful.

The Making of a Narcissistic Parent

Many narcissistic parents were themselves raised in environments of emotional neglect, conditional love, or rigid expectations. They were often praised for performance but punished for vulnerability.

Some were idealized as the "golden child" and learned to equate worth with success; others were humiliated and developed grandiosity as armor against shame. So when they become parents, they don't know how to love without control. This is also a reason why I think blaming them would not solve the root problem or will not promote your healing. They confuse attachment with possession, respect with obedience, and love with usefulness.

To the narcissistic parent, the child isn't a separate being with emotions and boundaries — the child is an *extension*. If the child behaves, achieves, or adores them, they feel powerful and validated. If the child defies, questions, or expresses pain, the parent feels threatened — and retaliates with withdrawal, criticism, or emotional punishment.

The relationship becomes a performance. The parent demands loyalty, admiration, and perfection, while the child learns to suppress authenticity in exchange for safety.

Different Faces of Narcissistic Parents

Not all narcissistic parents look the same.

Some are loud, commanding, and overtly self-absorbed; others are quiet, victimized, and manipulative in subtle ways. But the outcome for the child is always the same: emotional confusion and loss of self.

1. The Grandiose Narcissist

- Dominant, controlling, and dismissive.
- Expects admiration, obedience, and perfection.
- Uses fear, shame, or humiliation to maintain control.
- May boast about the child's achievements as trophies, but turns cold or cruel if the child fails to perform.

2. The Covert (or Vulnerable) Narcissist

- Appears sensitive, self-sacrificing, or even wounded.
- Plays the victim to manipulate guilt and sympathy.
- Creates emotional dependency — "I've done everything for you; how could you treat me this way?"

- Often weaponizes illness, sadness, or helplessness to control the child emotionally.

3. The Malignant Narcissist

- Combines narcissistic traits with aggression or sadism.
- Finds satisfaction in others' pain or fear.
- Engages in chronic manipulation, humiliation, and emotional abuse.
- It can cause deep trauma, hypervigilance, and complex PTSD in their children.

4. The Communal Narcissist

- Seeks admiration through altruism or social virtue.
- "Look how good a parent I am — everyone says so."
- Uses public kindness to mask private cruelty or neglect.
- Children often feel invalidated because no one believes their reality.

Regardless of type, the core theme remains:

The child exists to meet the parent's emotional needs, not the other way around.

The Family System

Narcissistic families operate like a performance troupe — everyone has a role, and breaking character comes with punishment. Some children become the Golden Child — idealized and used to reflect the parents' success.

Others become the Scapegoat — blamed for every problem, carrying the family's shame.

Some become the Lost Child, invisible and quiet, staying out of the line of fire.

And some become the Caretaker, trying to keep the peace, mediating conflicts, and soothing the parents' moods.

These roles are not chosen; they are assigned by the parent to preserve the illusion of control.

But even the Golden Child pays a price — they live in constant fear of falling from grace.

The Scapegoat bears rejection but often becomes the truth-teller later in life.

The Lost Child struggles to exist at all, and the Caretaker learns love means exhaustion. Personally speaking, I was the scapegoat and the caretaker. I received the blame for the family's problems, was targeted for criticism, punishment, or ridicule whenever my parent felt angry, insecure, or out of control. I was the one who saw the dysfunction and wouldn't pretend everything was perfect, and for that, I was punished or silenced. Any act of independence or self-expression from my side could trigger rejection or rage. Over time, I have internalized the belief that love must be earned through perfection, and peace only comes when I take the blame. At the same time, as the caretaker, I tried to soothe my parents' moods and learned to read emotional cues with hyper-awareness. I became sensitive, empathic, and responsible beyond my age. I unknowingly took on adult responsibilities too soon, feeling it was my job to hold the family together. I developed a strong helper identity, but often at the cost of my needs. Later, my needs became almost invisible even to myself. I tried to create emotional stability on my own by becoming the peacekeeper, the listener, the rescuer. Much later in life, I realized that it's a survival strategy, not a personality flaw.

I was blamed and needed at the same time. I subconsciously learned that love equals self-sacrifice and belonging means enduring pain. In my family, setting boundaries is considered selfish. I grew up with zero boundaries. As a result, a lot of people took advantage of me, and I was hurt and lonely during my college days. I also believed people who set boundaries were selfish.

The healing PATH

Healing means slowly dismantling those old roles. Remind yourself of these 4 truths.

1. Reclaim your identity beyond who you were in that family.
2. Release misplaced guilt — you were never responsible for fixing or saving a parent.
3. Learn self-compassion — the caretaker in you can now care for *yourself.*
4. Set boundaries — that's not betrayal; it's liberation.

Emotional Weapons: How Narcissistic Parents Control

Narcissistic parents use a predictable set of emotional weapons to maintain power.

Understanding them is the first step to disarming their effect.

1. Gaslighting

They deny or rewrite reality: "That never happened."

They make you question your memories, your feelings, even your sanity.

The goal: control your perception so you can no longer trust your truth.

2. Triangulation

They pit siblings, relatives, or friends against each other — creating rivalry and insecurity.

It ensures no one joins forces against them and keeps everyone competing for approval.

3. Emotional Invalidation

They dismiss your feelings: "You're too sensitive."

Over time, you stop expressing emotions at all, believing they're wrong or shameful.

4. Conditional Love

Love becomes transactional: "I love you when you make me proud."

Affection is earned, not given freely — teaching you that love must be *deserved*, not received.

5. Projection

They attribute their own flaws or insecurities to you:

If they are angry, you're "angry." If they're selfish, you're "ungrateful."

This keeps you defensive and confused, as you take responsibility for their emotional state.

6. Silent Treatment and Withdrawal

When displeased, they withhold affection, communication, or presence.

It's a form of punishment that says, "You don't exist until you obey."

Every interaction with a narcissistic parent follows a cycle:

1. Idealization – You are adored and praised. You feel seen, special, chosen.
2. Devaluation – The parent finds fault, criticizes, or withdraws love. You scramble to regain approval.
3. Discard or Re-engagement – They pull away or reappear, often acting as if nothing happened.

This constant push and pull conditions you to chase affection — a trauma bond disguised as loyalty. You learn to equate anxiety with love, unpredictability with passion, and silence with safety. This is dangerous, since as an adult you will always choose or subconsciously get attracted to individuals who are either narcissists, avoidant or anxious. Your brain is wired for the chase.

The Child's Adaptation: Surviving the Emotional Desert

Children in narcissistic homes adapt in brilliant, painful ways.

They learn to read moods, anticipate reactions, and avoid conflict.

They become hypervigilant — scanning every sigh, every tone, every shift in expression.

They often grow into adults who:

- Overanalyze others' feelings.
- Feel anxious when things are calm (waiting for the next storm).
- Struggle to trust that love can exist without performance.

This is the trauma of inconsistency — the parent who alternates between affection and cruelty, praise and punishment.

The child internalizes confusion: *If they sometimes love me, maybe I am the problem when they don't.* That confusion becomes the foundation of self-doubt — a defining wound of adult children of narcissistic parents.

The Cost: The Lost Self

When a child must constantly adapt to survive emotionally, their authentic self fades.

Their feelings, preferences, and boundaries get replaced by the parents' expectations.

You learn:

- To smile when you want to cry.
- To say "I'm fine" when you're hurting.
- To shrink when you should speak.

This loss of authenticity leads to an inner emptiness in adulthood.

You might find yourself asking:

"Who am I when no one else is watching?"

That question is the beginning of healing — because it means you're finally separating yourself from *them.*

Breaking the Blueprint

Healing begins when you see the pattern — not as destiny, but as programming.

You inherited a family blueprint built on shame, denial, and emotional control.

But it's not yours to carry.

You don't have to keep performing.

You don't have to earn love.

You don't have to keep replaying their story.

The narcissistic parent blueprint ends with awareness — and the decision to rewrite your own.

Now let's take some time to reflect on the following questions. (Remember, take your time, be gentle with yourself)

1. When did you first realize something was "off" in your relationship with your parent?
2. Which family role (Golden Child, Scapegoat, Lost Child, Caretaker) do you most identify with?

3. What messages about love, worth, or obedience were you taught that no longer serve you?
4. How does your body react when you imagine disappointing your parent — fear, guilt, shame, or relief?

Take your time, write freely, without judgment. This is where you begin to see your truth in black and white not through their eyes, but your own.

Chapter 3:
The Invisible Child

"You learned to disappear, just to survive."

The Childhood You Can't Remember

Many adult children of narcissistic parents describe their childhood as a blur.

Not because nothing happened, but because *too much* did. It's like memories exist behind a glass wall or are fragmented memories. Since your emotional reality is constantly denied, your mind learns to protect you by numbing out. Even when you try to talk to your relatives or friends about your parents, whether as a child or an adult, you are met with classic answers and advice like, "You shouldn't talk about your parents like this," "You should be thankful," or "They did their best." Now nowhere to go or anyone to understand you, you become a master at suppressing needs, smoothing conflict, and making yourself small enough to avoid notice. This is how the invisible child is born. Which I will talk about in a minute.

Another major concern is brain fog. Children of narcissistic parents often experience brain fog, both in childhood and adulthood. It's not "in their head" or a sign of weakness — it's a *real psychological and physiological response* to chronic emotional stress, confusion, and trauma. I particularly remember when I was 12 years old, my teacher asked me at lunchtime what I had for breakfast, and I couldn't remember. It felt strange, but I didn't know what to do. Such a situation, where I couldn't remember the time, occurred repeatedly. Even in my late 20s.

Brain fog is a nonmedical term that describes a range of cogni tive difficulties, including slowed thinking, poor concentration , mental fatigue, and cognitive impairment.[3]

Why Does It Happen in Children of Narcissistic Parents?

1. Chronic Emotional Hypervigilance

Your brain stays on high alert, trying to predict danger. This constant fight–flight–freeze activation floods your system with stress hormones like cortisol and adrenaline. *Is Mom angry? Is Dad about to explode? If I do this, will my parents be happy? Will they approve?*

Over time, this wears down cognitive clarity, and your brain prioritizes survival.

2. Gaslighting and Cognitive Dissonance

Narcissistic parents distort reality, they deny your experiences, twist the truth, or tell you what you saw or felt isn't real.

This creates cognitive dissonance, the mental tug-of-war between what you know and what you're told. Your brain learns to doubt its own perceptions. Eventually, thinking clearly becomes exhausting because you're always second-guessing yourself.

"Maybe it *was* my fault."

"Did that really happen?"

"Am I overreacting?"

This confusion *is* brain fog, a mental paralysis born from long-term invalidation.

3. Emotional Suppression and Dissociation

When your emotions were unsafe — mocked, punished, or ignored — your mind learned to shut down to survive.

You might have numbed out, detached, or gone "blank" in stressful moments.

That same mechanism in adulthood feels like zoning out, mental fatigue, or spacing — forms of dissociation, your brain's way of protecting you from emotional overload.

4. Lack of Emotional Mirroring and Validation

Children develop cognitive clarity through emotional validation — when parents help them name, understand, and regulate feelings.

Narcissistic parents, however, don't accurately reflect your emotions back; they make everything about themselves. Without that mirroring, the child grows up with fragmented self-awareness, unsure of who they are or how they feel.

That internal disconnection can manifest as mental fog or emotional confusion.

5. Exhaustion From Constant Self-Editing

You learned to walk on eggshells — monitoring every word, every facial expression, every tone to avoid conflict or rejection. That constant self-surveillance drains your cognitive energy. As an adult, it can feel like your mind is always tired, even when you've done nothing "stressful" in a typical sense.

Think of brain fog not as "brokenness," but as a pause your brain took to survive chaos. Remember it's not a sign of weakness, it's a sign of resilience.

How Invisibility Begins

In a narcissistic household, attention is a dangerous currency.

The spotlight belongs to the parent — their emotions, their image, their pain.

Children quickly learn that their own needs are inconvenient or threatening.

A few examples:

- *You cry, and they say, "Stop being dramatic. You're making me look bad."*
- *You succeed, and they say, "You think you're better than me?"*
- *You express hurt, and they reply, "After everything I've done for you?*

Every time you reach for connection, the door slams shut.

Over time, your system learns: *It's safer not to need. You try to become independent.* So you start to smile when you want to cry. You become polite, quiet, endlessly accommodating.

You convince yourself that wanting attention is selfish, that independence is a virtue, and that love must be earned. Over time you disappear in plain sight.

The Roles Within the Invisibility

Invisibility takes many shapes.

Some children become the Peacemakers — always smoothing conflict, always responsible for everyone's moods. Others become the Ghosts — quiet, unnoticed, blending into the walls.

And some become the Achievers — performing endlessly for recognition, but never truly seen for who they are.

No matter the variation, the message is the same:

Your visibility depends on their comfort. If you shine too brightly, they dim you.

If you speak the truth, they shame you. If you withdraw, they call you cold or ungrateful.

Whatever you do, it's wrong unless it serves their image.

Emotional Neglect: The Quietest Form of Abuse

Emotional neglect is often overlooked because it leaves no visible scars.

But for the invisible child, it's a constant hunger — for affection, attention, validation, or simple acknowledgment.

Neglect says:

"You don't matter."

"Your feelings are too much."

"Be who I need, not who you are."

Psychologically, this creates *emotional starvation.*

The brain and body learn to function with minimal emotional nourishment, surviving on scraps of approval. Research shows that children deprived of emotional responsiveness develop hypervigilance, anxiety, and identity confusion. These problems continue into adulthood.

They grow into adults who over-function in relationships, caretaking, fixing, rescuing — while ignoring their own exhaustion. Because once upon a time, their survival depended on staying invisible to avoid rejection or rage.

The Birth of the False Self

To survive emotional neglect, the invisible child creates a false self, a version of themselves that pleases the parent and keeps the peace, smiles, achieves, agrees, and apologizes.

It hides sadness, anger, disappointment, and even joy if those emotions threaten the parent's control. But beneath the false self-lives the true self — the part that still aches to be known, loved, and free. Psychologist D.W. Winnicott described this as a developmental adaptation:

When a child's authentic expressions are consistently met with disapproval or indifference, they build a protective mask. It keeps them safe, but at the cost of aliveness. You might feel this now, the constant sense of performing, of never being "enough," of wondering who you really are when you stop trying to please. That's not weakness; that's the residue of survival.

Why You Still Feel Invisible as an Adult

Even long after leaving the family home, the pattern continues.

You may notice yourself:

- Struggling to express needs without guilt.
- Overanalyzing others' moods to avoid conflict.
- Feeling invisible in relationships — unheard, unseen, or emotionally dismissed.
- Attracting partners or friends who repeat the same neglectful dynamic.

The brain, conditioned in childhood, seeks familiarity over safety.

It unconsciously recreates what it knows, even when it hurts.

That's why healing requires both awareness and reparenting:

You must teach yourself what healthy attention, validation, and emotional presence feel like. It begins with seeing *you.*

The Fear of Being Seen

Many invisible children fear visibility even as they crave it.

When you've been punished for existing, being noticed can feel dangerous. So you may sabotage opportunities, downplay achievements, or dismiss compliments.

You might even feel uncomfortable when someone truly listens — because part of you expects judgment or withdrawal to follow. This fear isn't irrational; it's learned.

In your family, attention came with strings attached. Praise was conditional. Vulnerability was ammunition. But now, as an adult, you have permission to unlearn that pattern.

You can practice safe visibility first with yourself, then with people who earn your trust.

Grieving the Unseen Childhood

There's a grief that comes with realizing you were never truly seen by your parents.

It's not just sadness; it's mourning for a life that could have been — for the laughter, comfort, and warmth you deserved but never received. You might feel anger, denial, guilt, or shame.

You might tell yourself, *"It wasn't that bad,"* or *"They did their best."*

But healing requires honesty: sometimes "their best" still caused harm. You are not disloyal for grieving the truth. You are reclaiming your right to have needs.

Steps Toward Visibility

1. Acknowledge the Pattern
2. Name it: "I learned to stay invisible to stay safe."
3. Awareness breaks the trance of self-blame.
4. Reconnect with Your Feelings
5. Ask yourself daily: *What am I feeling right now?*
6. It may take time for numbness to thaw. Be patient.
7. Express Needs Without Shame
8. Start small — ask for help, say no, or share preferences.

9. Your needs are not burdens; they are boundaries.
10. Choose Safe People
11. Surround yourself with those who see and respect you not for what you give, but for who you are.
12. Reparent Your Inner Child
13. Speak to the invisible child within you:
14. "I see you. You're allowed to exist. You matter."
15. This affirmation can slowly rewire years of invisibility.

Visibility as Healing

Visibility is not performance; it's presence.

It's learning to take up space without apology.

It's allowing your laughter to be loud, your sadness to be honored, and your boundaries to stand. Every time you let yourself be seen by yourself, by safe others, you weaken the old programming. You replace invisibility with authenticity. Healing doesn't mean you stop being quiet or gentle; it means your quietness is chosen, not enforced by fear.

Now let's take some time to reflect on the following questions. (Remember, take your time, be gentle with yourself)

1. When did you first learn that being seen or heard was unsafe?
2. How did you cope — by withdrawing, pleasing, performing, or staying silent?
3. What does invisibility feel like in your body? (tightness, numbness, tension, etc.)
4. When was the last time you felt truly *seen* — even for a moment? What was different about that experience?

5. What would “safe visibility” look like for you now?

You were never invisible because you lacked worth.

You became invisible because no one around you could bear your light. Now, you are the one who gets to see yourself — clearly, wholly, without shame.

Chapter 4:
The Rules of a Narcissistic Household

"In this house, truth is dangerous and silence is survival."

Your healing begins every time you let the invisible child step into the light.

The Unspoken Laws

Every narcissistic household runs on an invisible code — a set of unspoken rules designed to protect the parent's ego and maintain control. These rules are rarely said aloud, but they're felt in every glance, tone, and punishment. Children learn them early, sometimes before they can even speak. They become instinct. And breaking them, even unintentionally, comes with emotional consequences — ridicule, guilt, or icy withdrawal. You may not have realized it at the time, but you were living under psychological laws that dictated who you could be, what you could feel, and how much truth was allowed in the room. Let's name them — because naming what was hidden is the first act of freedom.

Rule #1: Don't Talk About It

The first and most sacred rule: *never expose the family's truth.*

What happens behind closed doors stays there.

You learn early that loyalty means silence, even if it costs your sanity. If you have ever tried to talk about the pain, you might have heard:

- "Why are you exaggerating?"
- "You're too sensitive."

- "We don't air dirty laundry."

This rule conditions you to doubt your perceptions and protect your parents' image at all costs.

It turns you into your own censor, editing your words, guarding your expressions, erasing your story. Even now, as an adult, you might feel anxious about speaking openly — afraid of judgment, guilt, or retaliation. But truth isn't betrayal. It's oxygen. Every time you speak honestly about your experience, you breathe life back into the parts of you that silence suffocated.

Rule #2: Don't Feel

Feelings threaten control.

In a narcissistic household, emotions are treated as weaknesses, inconveniences, or weapons.

If you cried, you were told to stop overreacting.

If you were angry, you were labeled disrespectful.

If you were joyful, you might have been accused of showing off.

So you learned to numb — to detach from your own internal world. Children who grow up under this rule often become adults who struggle to identify emotions. They know when others are upset, but not when *they* are. They intellectualize instead of feeling, analyze instead of crying, and distract instead of resting. But your emotions were never the problem. They were data messages from your body about what you needed, what hurt, and what mattered. Reconnecting with them is an act of rebellion and of healing.

Rule #3: Don't Trust

Trust is the foundation of safety.

But in a narcissistic family, trust is weaponized.

One day, your parent confides in you; the next, they use that same information to shame you. Promises are broken, boundaries violated, confidences exposed.

The message becomes clear: *No one is truly safe.* So you grow up cautious, guarded, and self-reliant. You double-check everyone's intentions. You read between the lines. You assume betrayal before it happens because it often does. Healing means learning that not everyone will use your vulnerability against you. It means building discernment instead of distrust — recognizing that trust isn't blindness, it's a choice. You can choose who earns it, one step at a time.

Rule #4: Don't Outshine the Parent

In narcissistic families, success is conditional.

You can be talented, but not *too* talented. Confident, but not *more* confident than the parent. If you excel, they may take credit or compete with you. If you fail, they may mock or reject you.

Either way, the focus returns to them their disappointment, their pride, their narrative. This rule creates a strange inner conflict: you crave achievement, but fear it at the same time.

You might downplay your accomplishments, sabotage opportunities, or feel guilty for wanting more. Breaking this rule means allowing yourself to shine without shame. You're not stealing light from anyone; you're reclaiming your own.

Rule #5: Keep the Parent Happy at All Costs

Every narcissistic household has a "weather system," and the parent is the storm.

Everyone learns to adjust to their moods, walking on eggshells, scanning for signs of danger, changing behavior to keep peace. You become the emotional regulator, soothing, apologizing, and fixing. You carry the weight of their disappointment and rage, believing it's your fault. This rule turns love into labor. You start to measure relationships by how much you can give, not how you're treated. But someone else's happiness was never your responsibility especially as a child.

You can care without caretaking. You can empathize without absorbing.

The healing phrase here is simple but radical:

"Their feelings are not my job."

Rule #6: Appear Perfect

Image is everything to a narcissistic parent. They may demand that the family appear flawless, smiling at gatherings, dressing neatly, and never revealing cracks. Behind the scenes, chaos reigns.

But in public, perfection must be maintained. This rule teaches children to perform. You become skilled at reading expectations and meeting them. Even as an adult, you might find yourself curating your life to look okay, struggling to admit when you're hurting. Perfectionism is a trauma response, an attempt to earn love through flawlessness. But authenticity is what heals. You don't have to be perfect to be worthy. You just have to be real.

Rule #7: The Parent Is Always Right

In a narcissistic household, the parents' authority is absolute. They rewrite history, deny wrongdoing, and twist logic until you question your memory. You learn that disagreeing means disrespecting. That boundaries mean betrayal. That truth is dangerous. This rule teaches submission disguised as respect. But real respect goes both ways, it honors reality. Breaking this rule requires courage to stand in your truth, even when they call it defiance. It's not rebellion; it's reclamation.

Rule #8: Love Equals Obedience

Perhaps the most painful rule of all: Love is conditional. You are loved when you please them.

You are ignored when you assert yourself. You are punished when you disagree. This trains your nervous system to associate love with compliance and fear with independence. In adulthood, this manifests as people-pleasing, codependency, and difficulty saying "no." You may confuse peace with silence and love with self-abandonment. Healing means redefining love as mutual respect, safety, and freedom, not control or approval.

The Emotional Consequences

These rules don't just shape behavior; they rewire the brain.

Children in narcissistic homes develop survival patterns:

- Hypervigilance: constant alertness to emotional danger.
- Fawning: appeasing to avoid rejection.
- Emotional numbness: disconnecting to endure pain.
- Chronic guilt: feeling responsible for others' emotions.

These responses keep you safe as a child but imprison you as an adult.

Healing begins when you recognize that these were never moral flaws, but survival strategies. You don't have to unlearn them overnight. You just have to learn that you have a choice now.

Breaking the Rules

Breaking the rules of a narcissistic household doesn't mean chaos; it means liberation.

You start small:

- Telling your story.
- Allowing yourself to feel.
- Trusting safe people.
- Letting yourself succeed.

- Saying “no” without explaining.

Each act of truth breaks one more link in the chain. At first, it feels terrifying — your nervous system expects punishment. But over time, you realize the world doesn’t collapse when you stop obeying lies. Freedom feels strange at first, then beautiful.

Now let’s take some time to reflect on the following questions. (Remember take your time, be gentle with yourself)

1. Which of these rules feels most familiar to you?
2. What happened when you broke a rule as a child?
3. Which rule do you still unconsciously follow in adult life?
4. What would it look like to live without that rule today?

You didn’t fail your family by breaking their rules.

Their rules failed to nurture your humanity. Every time you choose honesty over silence, feeling over fear, authenticity over approval, you are rewriting the family code. And this time, the only rule is truth. And ye shall know the truth, and the truth shall make you free. John 8:32 KJV.

Chapter 5:
Gaslighting, Denial, and Reality Confusion

"If you can't trust your own eyes, you can't trust yourself."

The Mechanics of Gaslighting

Gaslighting is one of the cruelest tools a narcissistic parent wields.

It's not just lying, it's the systematic distortion of reality to control perception, manipulate emotions, and maintain authority. From a young age, you are subtly (or overtly) trained to doubt your memory, your instincts, and your feelings.

You may remember vividly:

- "That never happened."
- "You're imagining things."
- "You're too sensitive."

At first, you hesitate. Maybe it *didn't* happen the way you think. Maybe you *are* overreacting.

By the time you reach adulthood, this self-doubt is embedded as a constant whisper: *Am I wrong? Did I do something to deserve this?* Gaslighting isn't random. It's strategic. It keeps the child and later the adult off balance. When your reality is questioned repeatedly, the narcissist controls the narrative, the emotions, and the outcome.

Everyday Examples of Gaslighting

Gaslighting can be subtle or extreme, verbal or behavioral. Here are some common forms:

1. **Denying Your Experience**
    - You remember an event clearly. They say, "That's not what happened. You're exaggerating."
    - Your brain hesitates: Did it happen, or am I misremembering?
2. **Minimizing Your Feelings**
    - "You're overreacting."
    - "Stop being dramatic."
    - "It wasn't that bad."
    - You internalize: *Maybe I am too sensitive. Maybe my feelings are wrong.*
3. **Blaming You for Their Actions**
    - "I only yelled because you made me do it."
    - "If you hadn't been so difficult, I wouldn't have snapped."
    - You begin to feel responsible for their emotions and behavior.
4. **Twisting Facts or Events**
    - "You said this, but you meant that."
    - "I never said that."
    - Memories you trusted become suspect.
5. **Isolating You from Truth**
    - Other family members or friends are brought in to confirm their version.
    - You learn *that no one will back you up. I am alone in my perception.*

6. **Silent Treatment or Withdrawal**
    - When you protest or speak your truth, they retreat or act coldly.
    - The unspoken message: *If you keep insisting, you will be punished*

The Emotional Fallout

The consequences of prolonged gaslighting are profound:

- Chronic Self-Doubt

  Your brain learns to second-guess itself. You may replay conversations endlessly, question your memory, or apologize when you've done nothing wrong.

- Anxiety and Hypervigilance

  You constantly scan for signs of disapproval or manipulation, trying to anticipate danger.

- Shame and Guilt

  You may feel defective simply for having needs, opinions, or emotions.

- Identity Confusion

  Over time, you may ask: *Who am I, independent of their version of me?*

- Emotional Dysregulation

  Your nervous system learned that feelings trigger punishment, so you might overreact, underreact, or suppress emotions altogether.

These patterns persist into adulthood, affecting relationships, work, and self-esteem. The Cycle of Denial

Narcissistic parents often combine gaslighting with denial.

- Rewriting History: They may insist events occurred differently, or never at all.
- Shifting Blame: You become the villain in your own story.
- Invalidating Reality: Even your memories and perceptions are questioned, leaving you uncertain about what is true.

Denial strengthens control. If you can't trust your own experience, you are more likely to comply with theirs. It's exhausting like trying to navigate a labyrinth with no map, where the walls shift constantly.

The Inner Split: Self vs. Parent

Living with gaslighting creates a split inside. One part of you remembers clearly, senses danger, and feels hurt. The other part doubts, rationalizes, and apologizes. This inner conflict is exhausting and isolating. You may feel like two people in one body:

- The child who knows the truth.
- The child who fears punishment for speaking it.

Healing requires reintegration, trusting the part of yourself that felt, remembered, and recognized injustice.

Reclaiming Your Reality

Breaking free from gaslighting begins with validation.

1. **Trust Your Memories**
    - Record events in a journal.
    - Write down feelings and perceptions without judgment.
    - Over time, the evidence of your reality becomes undeniable.

2. **Notice Emotional Reactions**
    - Your body knows the truth before your mind does.
    - Anxiety, tightness, or gut instincts often signal gaslighting — not overreaction.
3. **Seek External Confirmation**
    - Talk to safe friends, therapists, or support groups.
    - Their acknowledgment reinforces your sense of reality.
4. **Name the Behavior**
    - "That was gaslighting."
    - Naming it empowers you to separate the behavior from yourself.
5. **Set Mental Boundaries**
    - Remind yourself: I do not have to accept their version of reality.
    - You can observe, disengage, and preserve your truth.

Reconnecting with Intuition

Decades of gaslighting teach the mind to distrust itself.

Rebuilding trust requires practice:

- Pause before you react to criticism or manipulation.
- Check in with your feelings: *Does this feel right to me?*
- Affirm your own perspective: *I remember this differently, and my experience is valid.*
- Celebrate small victories — trusting yourself in minor decisions — to reinforce confidence.

Your intuition is not broken. It was silenced. And it is waking up.

Now let's take some time to reflect on the following questions. (Remember, take your time, be gentle with yourself)

1. Can you identify moments in your childhood where your perception was denied or questioned?
2. How do you feel physically and emotionally when someone challenges your memory or emotions today?
3. What truths have you ignored about your childhood to avoid conflict?
4. How can you begin to validate your reality in small ways every day?
5. Write a letter to your inner child, affirming their memory, feelings, and perspective.

Gaslighting and denial are not signs of weakness in you.

They are survival mechanisms and adaptations that kept you safe in an unsafe environment. Reclaiming your reality is an act of courage.

It is the first step in undoing the control that shaped your sense of self.

Every time you remember, feel, and assert your truth, you dismantle the illusion that has held you captive. Your mind is yours again. Your perception is yours again.

And with that freedom, healing becomes possible.

Chapter 6:
The Adult Child's Core Wounds

"The scars aren't always visible, but they shape everything you do."

The Lasting Imprint of Narcissistic Parenting

Growing up with a narcissistic parent doesn't just affect your childhood; it leaves an enduring blueprint that shapes your adult life. Even after you leave the family home, the lessons of survival remain: self-doubt, guilt, perfectionism, anxiety, and relational challenges. These patterns aren't your fault; they are the emotional residue of adapting to a household that demanded your compliance, invisibility, or constant appeasement. They are the core wounds carried by adult children of narcissists.

Core Wound #1: Chronic Self-Doubt

When your feelings, thoughts, and perceptions were constantly questioned or dismissed, self-doubt became ingrained.

You might find yourself:

- Overthinking every decision.
- Second-guessing your intuition.
- Apologizing excessively.

Self-doubt isn't laziness or incompetence. It's a learned survival strategy, your nervous system is saying: *I must be careful. I cannot trust myself.* Healing begins with conscious affirmation: noticing when doubt arises and gently reminding yourself that your thoughts and feelings are valid.

Core Wound #2: People-Pleasing and Approval Seeking

To survive emotional volatility, you likely became adept at predicting others' needs, moods, and expectations.

This translates into adulthood as people-pleasing:

- Saying yes when you want to say no.
- Prioritizing others' comfort over your own is important.
- Seeking external validation to feel worthy.

The adult child learns that love, safety, and acceptance are conditional, so we chase them endlessly, even at our own expense.

Breaking free requires:

- Learning to set boundaries without guilt.
- Accepting that self-worth is inherent, not earned, is important.
- Practicing small acts of self-affirmation daily.

Core Wound #3: Perfectionism and Hyper-Responsibility

Many adult children of narcissists develop perfectionism as armor:

- You overprepare, overachieve, or overcompensate.
- Mistakes feel catastrophic, even when minor.
- Responsibility for others' feelings becomes your default role.

Perfectionism is rooted in the belief that love and safety must be earned through performance.

Recovery involves embracing imperfection as a human right, allowing yourself to fail, rest, and exist without constant justification.

Core Wound #4: Boundary Confusion

Narcissistic parents rarely respect boundaries.

- Your space, time, feelings, and opinions were overridden or ignored.
- Requests for privacy or autonomy were met with guilt, rage, or manipulation.

As an adult, you may struggle to recognize or assert boundaries:

- Saying no feels disloyal.
- Defending your needs feels selfish.
- Toxic people can easily cross your limits because your nervous system still expects violation.

Healing requires explicit practice: naming boundaries, stating them clearly, and protecting them without apology.

Core Wound #5: Shame and Guilt

Shame is the internalized voice of the narcissistic parent.

Guilt often accompanies it, teaching you that taking care of yourself is selfish.

- You feel embarrassed about needs, desires, or mistakes.
- You carry an exaggerated sense of responsibility for others' emotions.
- You replay old conflicts, apologizing in your mind long after the event.

Recovery involves distinguishing healthy guilt (awareness and growth) from toxic guilt (conditioned shame imposed by the parent).

Core Wound #6: Identity Confusion

Perhaps the most pervasive wound is the loss of authentic self.

- Who are you when you stop performing for approval?
- Which feelings, opinions, or desires are genuinely yours?

Many adult children feel like strangers to themselves.

This is the false self-created to survive parental control, fighting silently with the true self the part longing for authenticity, freedom, and love without strings. Reclaiming identity is central to healing: rediscovering passions, desires, values, and beliefs that were suppressed or denied.

Core Wound #7: Relationship Challenges

The impact of these wounds extends into adulthood relationships:

- You attract partners who mirror parental dynamics — critical, controlling, or emotionally distant.
- Intimacy triggers fear because vulnerability once invited punishment.
- You may over function, over care, or tolerate abuse to maintain connection.

Healing requires conscious awareness of patterns and learning new relational skills:

- Choosing partners who respect boundaries.
- Allowing emotional reciprocity.
- Listening to your intuition instead of old survival strategies.

Healing the Core Wounds

1. Awareness

   Naming the wounds is the first step. Understanding that these patterns are conditioned responses — not moral flaws — is liberating.

2. Self-Compassion

   Treat yourself as you would a child who survived impossible conditions. Be gentle with mistakes, fear, and old coping mechanisms.

3. Reparenting the Inner Child

   - Speak to the child who needed validation and safety.
   - Affirm that they were not at fault.
   - Provide the love and guidance that was missing.

4. Therapy and Support

   Professional guidance can help process trauma, restructure cognitive distortions, and learn relational skills. Support groups and books can normalize your experience and reduce isolation.

5. Boundary Practice

   Start small: say no to minor requests, take your needs seriously, and assert personal limits. Growth occurs in incremental steps.

Authenticity Exercises

Explore passions, hobbies, and preferences that were suppressed. Gradually integrate these into your life without guilt.

Now let's take some time to reflect on the following questions. (Remember, take your time, be gentle with yourself)

1. Which of these core wounds resonates most with you?
2. How do these wounds show up in your current life — in relationships, work, or self-perception?
3. What coping mechanisms did you develop to survive childhood that no longer serve you?
4. What small steps can you take today to nurture the adult self you were denied?

The wounds left by narcissistic parenting are deep, but they are not permanent.

They shaped your survival, not your destiny. Every time you acknowledge your truth, set a boundary, or choose self-care over obligation, you chip away at the old conditioning.

You are not broken. You were adapting. Healing is not linear, and it requires courage, patience, and consistency. But each step brings you closer to reclaiming your mind, heart, and identity.

Chapter 7:
Boundaries, Assertiveness, and Saying No

"You are allowed to exist on your own terms."

Why Boundaries Are Revolutionary for Adult Children of Narcissists

If you grew up with a narcissistic parent, boundaries may feel foreign, even selfish.

You were taught that protecting yourself, asserting needs, or saying no would provoke anger, withdrawal, or guilt. Setting boundaries is not rebellion; it is self-preservation. It is the first step toward reclaiming autonomy and a sense of safety in relationships. Boundaries are the invisible fences that define where you end and another begins — emotionally, mentally, and physically.

Without them, you are vulnerable to manipulation, over-responsibility, and self-neglect.

Boundaries: When To Say Yes, How to Say No. A book by Dr. **Henry Cloud**, Dr. **John Townsend** is a great book which talks about healthy boundaries in all relationships[4]. The Types of Boundaries

1. Emotional Boundaries
    - Protect your feelings from being controlled or dismissed.
    - Examples: refusing to accept blame for another's anger, not tolerating verbal abuse, acknowledging your emotions as valid.

2. Physical Boundaries
    - Protect your body, space, and privacy.
    - Examples: choosing who can touch you, deciding when you need personal space, and controlling your living environment.
3. Time Boundaries
    - Protect your energy and availability.
    - Examples: saying no to constant demands, allocating time for rest and hobbies, and prioritizing personal projects.
4. Intellectual Boundaries
    - Protect your thoughts and beliefs.
    - Examples: refusing to be shamed for opinions, not debating endlessly to please others, and asserting knowledge without apology.
5. Material Boundaries
    - Protect your possessions and resources.
    - Examples: refusing to lend money you can't afford to lose, deciding what you share with others, and keeping personal items secure.

The Fear Behind Saying No

Many adult children of narcissists hesitate to say no because:

- They fear anger or punishment.
- They feel guilt for disappointing others.
- They worry about being abandoned or unloved.

These fears are echoes of childhood conditioning. Your nervous system associates saying no with danger even when the risk no longer exists. The truth: Saying no does not make you bad. It makes you human. Boundaries protect your well-being and are essential for healthy relationships.

Assertiveness: The Skill of Speaking Your Truth

Assertiveness is the ability to express your thoughts, feelings, and needs clearly and respectfully.

It is different from aggression (violating others' rights) or passivity (violating your own).

- Passive: "I guess it's fine if you do it this way."
- Aggressive: "You must do it my way!"
- Assertive: "I'm not comfortable with that. Here's what I need."

Assertiveness communicates self-respect. It sets the tone that your needs matter and encourages others to honor them.

Practical Steps to Build Assertiveness

1. Identify Your Needs
   - Start small: What do you need today to feel safe, respected, or valued?
2. Use "I" Statements
   - Focus on your experience instead of blaming:
   - *"I feel overwhelmed when I'm interrupted. Please let me finish."*
3. Practice Saying No
   - Start with low-risk situations.
   - Gradually work toward bigger, emotionally charged requests.
4. Set Clear Consequences
   - Boundaries are only effective if they are enforceable.

- Example: *"If you continue to shout, I will leave the room."*

5. Stay Calm and Consistent
    - Narcissistic patterns may provoke resistance or guilt-tripping.
    - Consistency teaches others that your boundaries are non-negotiable.

The Emotional Experience of Boundaries

When you first assert yourself, you may feel:

- Guilt: Old survival patterns tell you you're being selfish.
- Fear: Anxiety about rejection, anger, or retaliation.
- Relief: A sense of empowerment and safety.
- Anger: Recognition of past violations.

All of these emotions are normal. Feeling them does not mean you did the wrong thing. It means you are reclaiming autonomy. Boundaries are not just about keeping others out; they are about defining where you begin and end.

They allow for:

- Healthier friendships that respect your time and energy.
- Romantic relationships are built on mutual respect, not dependency.
- Family interactions where you can engage without losing yourself are important.

Remember: Some relationships may resist your new boundaries. Some people may attempt to manipulate or guilt you. This is natural, especially if your boundaries challenge old patterns. Your responsibility is to maintain them, not to control their reaction.

Reclaiming Your Voice

Adult children of narcissists often struggle to speak up because their voice was suppressed.

Reclaiming it requires practice:

- Start by expressing opinions in safe spaces.
- Gradually share needs with supportive friends or therapists.
- Record progress in a journal: *Today, I said no. Today I asked for what I needed.*

Your voice is your power. Every time you use it to honor your truth, you chip away at the programming of compliance and fear.

Now let's take some time to reflect on the following questions. (Remember, take your time, be gentle with yourself)

1. Which boundaries do you struggle to assert most, and why?
2. When was the last time you said no, and how did it feel?
3. What is one small boundary you can practice today?
4. How does guilt show up when you honor yourself, and how can you reframe it as self-care?
5. Who in your life respects your boundaries, and who challenges them? How will you respond?

Always remember, setting boundaries is not just an act of self-preservation, it is an act of self-love. Assertiveness is not aggression; it is clarity, honesty, and respect. Every "no" you speak with confidence, every boundary you enforce, every truth you assert is a brick in the foundation of your autonomy. You are allowed to take up space. You are allowed to protect yourself. You are allowed to exist fully, freely, and authentically.

Chapter 8:
Healing Through Self-Compassion and Inner Child Work

"The child you once protected now deserves your care."

Why Self-Compassion Matters

Adult children of narcissistic parents often carry shame, self-criticism, and relentless self-judgment. These patterns are survival mechanisms from childhood, designed to keep you small, quiet, and compliant. Self-compassion is the antidote. It is the practice of treating yourself with the same kindness, understanding, and patience you would offer a child who was hurt. It is not indulgence. It is not a weakness. It is reclaiming the care you were denied.

The Inner Child: Who Are They?

The inner child is the part of you that experienced neglect, fear, or emotional invalidation.

This child:

- Felt unseen, unheard, or unworthy.
- Learned to survive by disappearing, pleasing, or numbing.
- Still carries the longing for validation, love, and safety.

Healing begins by acknowledging this child, listening to their needs, and offering consistent care.

Connecting With Your Inner Child

1. Visualize the Child Within

- Close your eyes and picture yourself at age 5–10.
- Observe their expressions, posture, and emotions.
- Don't judge; simply notice.

2. Speak With Kindness
   - Say aloud or silently: "I see you. I hear you. You were not at fault. You are safe now."
3. Validate Feelings
   - If the child feels anger, sadness, or fear, respond with acceptance:
   - *"It's okay to feel this. Your feelings are real and important."*
4. Offer Protection and Comfort
   - Imagine holding them, providing warmth, safety, and reassurance.
   - Reinforce the idea that they are now in an environment where they can heal.

Self-Compassion Exercises

1. The Loving-Kindness Practice
   - Close your eyes.
   - Repeat: *"May I be safe. May I be happy. May I be healthy. May I live with ease."*
   - Extend this compassion to your inner child: *"May you be seen. May you be loved. May you be free."*
2. Journaling Letters
   - Write letters to your inner child.
   - Acknowledge pain, validate feelings, and offer encouragement.

    - Example: *"Dear little me, I know you were scared and alone. I am here now, and I will never leave you unheard."*

3. Compassionate Self-Talk
    - Catch self-critical thoughts and reframe them:
        - Instead of: "I'm weak for feeling this," say: "I am human, and it's okay to feel."
    - Speak to yourself as a nurturing parent would.
4. Safe Space Visualization
    - Create a mental sanctuary where your inner child feels protected.
    - Include comforting elements: a warm blanket, favorite toys, sunlight, or a gentle companion.
    - Visit this space whenever anxiety, shame, or self-doubt arises.

Undoing the Effects of Emotional Neglect

Narcissistic parenting often leaves adults emotionally undernourished.

Inner child work and self-compassion fill the gaps:

- Acknowledgment: Recognize the neglect and its impact.
- Validation: Confirm your feelings were valid, even if they were dismissed.
- Protection: Set boundaries to prevent ongoing harm.
- Nurturing: Provide consistent care, love, and encouragement to the inner child.

These practices help rewire your nervous system, restoring safety, self-worth, and emotional resilience.

Integration Into Daily Life

- Morning Affirmations: Start the day by reminding yourself: *"I am worthy. I am enough. I will care for myself today."*
- Check-Ins: Pause during stressful moments to ask your inner child: *"What do you need right now?"*
- Celebrate Small Wins: Acknowledge progress — whether it's asserting a boundary, expressing a feeling, or practicing self-kindness.

Healing is cumulative. Each act of self-compassion strengthens your capacity to trust yourself, feel deeply, and live authentically.

Now let's take some time to reflect on the following questions. (Remember, take your time, be gentle with yourself)

1. What messages did your inner child receive growing up?
2. How did you cope with neglect or invalidation as a child?
3. How can you respond to your inner child with compassion today?
4. What daily practices can remind you that you are safe, seen, and loved?
5. How does nurturing your inner child change your adult self-perception?

The child you once had to protect, silence, or ignore now lives within you.

They deserve kindness, validation, and care, not because you failed as a child, but because survival demanded it. Every time you acknowledge their pain, speak compassionately, or offer reassurance, you heal a piece of the self that was once wounded. Healing is not forgetting. Healing is giving that child and yourself what you always deserved: love, safety, and permission to exist fully.

Chapter 9:
Rebuilding Self-Esteem and Personal Identity

"You are not who they told you to be —you are who you choose to become."

Why Self-Esteem Falters in Adult Children of Narcissists

Growing up with narcissistic parents often distorts your sense of self-worth.

- Love was conditional, based on performance or compliance.
- Criticism and invalidation taught you that your thoughts, feelings, and achievements were never enough.
- Praise was rare, inconsistent, or manipulative.

As an adult, this can manifest as:

- Persistent self-doubt.
- Reluctance to accept compliments.
- Fear of pursuing ambitions.
- Overdependence on external validation.

Your self-esteem may feel fragile, easily shaken by criticism, rejection, or failure.

Rebuilding it begins with understanding that your value was never determined by their approval.

Separating Self-Worth from Parental Validation

The first step toward reclaiming self-esteem is disentangling your worth from external approval:

- Recognize the Source of the Lie
- *"I was not valued as a child, but that does not define me as an adult."*
- Affirm Your Intrinsic Value
    - o You exist; therefore, you are worthy.
    - o Your needs, feelings, and desires are valid, independent of anyone's recognition.
- Replace Conditional Approval with Self-Validation
    - o Instead of: "I am good if they approve me"
    - o Say: "I am good because I am alive, learning, and trying."

Practical Strategies to Rebuild Self-Esteem

1. Celebrate Small Wins

- Record daily accomplishments, no matter how minor.
- Examples include cooking a meal, asserting a boundary, and completing a task.
- These accumulate and reinforce self-efficacy.

2. Affirm Your Strengths

- List qualities, talents, and achievements.
- Revisit this list daily.
- Focus on *who you are*, not only what you do.

3. **Challenge Negative Self-Talk**
    - Identify self-critical thoughts.
    - Ask: *Is this true? Would I say this to someone I love?*
    - Reframe: *"I am learning. I am allowed to make mistakes."*
4. **Set Achievable Goals**
    - Pursue personal goals that reflect your values, not others' expectations.
    - Break larger ambitions into small, manageable steps.
    - Progress, not perfection, reinforces self-worth.
5. **Build Supportive Relationships**
    - Surround yourself with people who see, respect, and uplift you.
    - Avoid relationships that replicate narcissistic dynamics.

Rediscovering Personal Identity

Adult children of narcissists often struggle to know who they are outside parental influence.

- The "false self" may dominate the version that appeased, performed, or adapted.
- The "true self" may feel hidden, unsure, or unworthy.

Reclaiming identity involves:

1. Exploration
    - Experiment with hobbies, beliefs, and activities that were discouraged or ignored.
    - Notice what excites, energizes, or fulfills you.

2. Authenticity
    - Express your opinions, preferences, and emotions without apology.
    - Small acts of authenticity rebuild trust in yourself.
3. Reflection
    - Ask: Who am I beyond family expectations?
    - Journal your thoughts, dreams, and insights.
4. Integration
    - Allow the inner child and adult self to coexist.
    - Align values, actions, and self-expression.

The Role of Self-Compassion in Identity Building

Self-esteem grows strongest when paired with self-compassion:

- Treat yourself gently during failures or setbacks.
- Affirm that growth is a process, not a final destination.
- Recognize that reclaiming identity may provoke normal discomfort.

Overcoming the Fear of Being Seen

Many adult children fear visibility because:

- Criticism or ridicule conditioned avoidance.
- Being seen may feel risky or uncomfortable.

Strategies to embrace visibility:

1. Start small: share thoughts, feelings, or opinions in safe settings.
2. Celebrate vulnerability: notice courage, not outcomes.

3. Reflect: *My worth is inherent, not dependent on others' reactions.*

Over time, the fear diminishes, replaced by empowerment and authenticity.

Now let's take some time to reflect on the following questions. (Remember, take your time, be gentle with yourself)

1. Which parts of your identity feel most authentic today?
2. Which aspects were shaped primarily by parental expectations?
3. How can you nurture your authentic self in everyday life?
4. What strengths and talents have you overlooked or minimized?
5. What small steps can you take to assert your true identity this week?

Self-esteem and personal identity are not gifts you receive; they are rights you reclaim.

Each act of authenticity, each boundary, each affirmation of your value chips away at the old conditioning. You are not the child who had to survive a narcissistic parent.

You are an adult with the power to define yourself, honor your truth, and live unapologetically.

Chapter 10:
Healthy Relationships After Narcissistic Parenting

"You can love and be loved without losing yourself."

Why Relationships Are Challenging for Adult Children of Narcissists

Growing up with a narcissistic parent shape how you relate to others:

- You may attract partners or friends who replicate familiar dynamics — critical, controlling, or emotionally unavailable.
- You may over-function to maintain peace, approval, or connection.
- You may struggle to trust, fearing manipulation, rejection, or betrayal.

These patterns are normal responses to childhood conditioning, but they don't have to define your adult life.

Red Flags to Recognize

When rebuilding relationships, it helps to identify warning signs early:

1. Control or Domination
    - o A partner or friend tries to dictate your choices, appearance, or behavior.

2. Constant Criticism
    - Subtle or overt attacks on your thoughts, feelings, or achievements.
3. Boundary Violation
    - Ignoring "no," pressuring, or disregarding your needs and space.
4. Emotional Unavailability
    - Lack of empathy, support, or emotional reciprocity.
5. Gaslighting or Manipulation
    - Denying facts, minimizing feelings, or twisting events to make you doubt yourself.

Recognizing these patterns helps prevent repeating childhood dynamics.

The Foundations of Healthy Relationships

1. Mutual Respect
    - Both parties honor boundaries, feelings, and individuality.
2. Clear Communication
    - Opinions, needs, and concerns are expressed openly without fear of retaliation.
3. Emotional Reciprocity
    - Both partners offer and receive support, care, and validation.
4. Trust and Safety
    - Confidence that vulnerability will not be weaponized.

5. Autonomy Within Connection
    - Each person maintains identity, interests, and personal space.

Healthy relationships allow growth, connection, and intimacy without the sacrifice of self.

Strategies for Building Healthy Relationships

1. Start With Self-Knowledge
    - Understand your values, needs, and boundaries.
    - Be clear on what is non-negotiable for your well-being.
2. Set and Enforce Boundaries Early
    - Communicate limits gently but firmly.
    - Respect yourself enough to step away if boundaries are violated.
3. Observe Patterns, Not Appearances
    - Charm or attentiveness may hide manipulation.
    - Look for consistency in words, actions, and respect for boundaries.
4. Prioritize Emotional Safety
    - Trust your intuition.
    - Notice if interactions leave you anxious, drained, or diminished.
5. Practice Vulnerability Gradually
    - Share feelings and experiences incrementally.
    - Gauge responses: supportive behavior signals a healthy connection.

6. Seek Support
    - Trusted friends, therapists, or support groups provide perspective and reassurance.

Romantic Relationships

Adult children of narcissists often face challenges like:

- Fear of abandonment or over-attachment.
- Repeating family patterns with controlling or critical partners.
- Difficulty asserting needs or saying no.

Healthy romantic partnerships require:

- Equality and respect.
- Clear emotional boundaries.
- Open and honest communication.
- Space for individual growth.

It may take time to unlearn the instinct to prioritize a partner's needs over your own, but practice strengthens independence and intimacy simultaneously.

Friendships and Social Connections

Friendships can also mirror old patterns if boundaries are weak:

- Avoid friends who exploit, manipulate, or demean you.
- Seek connections that are supportive, reciprocal, and respectful.
- Practice saying no to requests that drain your energy.

Friendships should feel safe, energizing, and validating — not conditional or fearful.

Family Dynamics After Narcissistic Parenting

Engaging with family can be complicated:

- Limited contact or no contact may be necessary for emotional safety.
- Boundaries must be reinforced, even with relatives.
- Accept that some family members may resist change or refuse to respect your autonomy.

Remember: you are not obligated to endure toxic behavior for the sake of tradition or guilt.

Rewriting the Relationship Blueprint

You have the power to define what relationships look like:

- You can expect respect and empathy.
- You can prioritize your needs and voice.
- You can leave connections that undermine your mental and emotional health.

Healthy relationships are not earned; they are mutual.

They are built on shared values, respect, and safety — not survival, fear, or obligation.

Now let's take some time to reflect on the following questions. (Remember, take your time, be gentle with yourself)

1. Which relationships in your life feel safe and supportive?
2. Where do you notice old patterns of over-functioning, people-pleasing, or fear?
3. What boundaries could you enforce today to protect your well-being?

4. Are there relationships you need to distance yourself from for emotional health?
5. How can you practice vulnerability safely with trusted individuals?

You are allowed to have relationships that nourish, respect, and empower you.

You do not need to tolerate manipulation, control, or disrespect to maintain a connection. Every time you assert boundaries, communicate openly, and prioritize your needs, you strengthen your ability to attract and maintain healthy, loving connections. Healthy relationships are possible, and you deserve them.

Chapter 11:
Self-Care and Emotional Regulation

"Caring for yourself is not selfish — it's survival and healing."

Why Self-Care Is Crucial for Adult Children of Narcissists

Growing up with a narcissistic parent often conditions you to prioritize others' needs over your own.

- Your energy was spent managing the parents' emotions.
- Your feelings were minimized or invalidated.
- Your survival depended on self-neglect and vigilance.

As an adult, these patterns can manifest as:

- Chronic exhaustion, burnout, or anxiety.
- Difficulty identifying your own needs.
- Feeling guilty for prioritizing yourself.

Self-care is the antidote — a conscious reclaiming of energy, autonomy, and emotional balance.

Understanding Emotional Dysregulation

Emotional dysregulation is common in adult children of narcissists.

- You may overreact to minor triggers.
- You may suppress emotions until they explode.
- Anxiety, guilt, or shame may dominate responses.

These patterns are remnants of a childhood where emotions were unsafe or manipulated.

Learning to regulate emotions is not suppression; it is awareness, acceptance, and skillful response.

Foundations of Emotional Regulation

1. Awareness
    - Notice emotional reactions as they arise.
    - Identify the triggers: past wounds, current stress, or unmet needs.
2. Validation
    - Acknowledge your feelings without judgment: *"I am anxious, and that's understandable."*
3. Grounding Techniques
    - Focus on the present moment to calm the nervous system.
    - Examples: deep breathing, body scans, sensory grounding (touch, sound, smell).
4. Cognitive Reframing
    - Challenge negative or automatic thoughts.
    - Ask: *Is this thought factual? Is it helpful?*
5. Self-Compassion
    - Treat yourself gently during emotional turbulence.
    - Remind yourself: *This is a learned response, and I am learning new ways to cope.*

Daily Self-Care Practices

1. Physical Self-Care
    - Sleep, nutrition, and exercise support emotional stability.
    - Even small routines, such as a short walk, stretching, or balanced meals, restore energy.
2. Emotional Self-Care
    - Journal your feelings to process and release emotions.
    - Allow yourself to cry, laugh, or vent safely.
    - Engage in activities that bring joy and relaxation.
3. Mental Self-Care
    - Limit exposure to toxic people, media, or environments.
    - Practice mindfulness, meditation, or reading for growth.
    - Challenge self-critical or perfectionistic thinking.
4. Spiritual Self-Care (if applicable)
    - Connect with your beliefs, values, or purpose.
    - Engage in practices that nurture your sense of meaning.

Practical Techniques for Emotional Regulation

- Box Breathing
    - Inhale for 4 counts, hold for 4, exhale for 4, hold for 4.
    - Repeat to calm the nervous system during anxiety or overwhelm.
- Grounding with the Senses
    - Name 5 things you see, 4 you feel, 3 you hear, 2 you smell, 1 you taste.

    - Anchors you in the present, reducing emotional flooding.
- Emotion Labeling
    - Name what you feel: “I am frustrated and anxious.”
    - Labeling reduces intensity and creates clarity.
- Safe Space Visualization
    - Imagine a secure, calming environment where you feel protected.
    - Visit this space mentally when triggered or exhausted.
- Daily Reflection
    - Journal moments of emotional strength, boundary assertion, or self-care.
    - Track growth and reinforce progress.

Overcoming Guilt Around Self-Care

Guilt is a common barrier:

- Childhood taught you that attending to your needs was selfish.
- Self-care may feel indulgent, unnecessary, or wrong.

Reframe: Self-care is not selfish. It is the foundation for health, healing, and sustainable relationships.

Your energy, presence, and effectiveness depend on it.

Now let’s take some time to reflect on the following questions. (Remember, take your time, be gentle with yourself)

1. How often do you prioritize your own needs?

2. Which self-care practices feel most accessible or appealing to you?
3. What guilt arises when you focus on yourself, and how can you reframe it?
4. How do you notice emotional dysregulation showing up in daily life?
5. Which grounding or emotional regulation techniques can you practice this week?

Self-care and emotional regulation are the pillars that sustain healing and autonomy.

By protecting your energy, honoring your feelings, and practicing daily self-compassion, you reclaim the parts of yourself that were silenced or neglected.

Every act of care, no matter how small, is a declaration: *I matter. My emotions matter. My well-being matters*

Chapter 12: Forgiveness, Acceptance, and Moving Forward

"Freedom begins when you release the weight of what was never yours to carry."

Redefining Forgiveness

For adult children of narcissists, forgiveness is often misunderstood:

- It is not excusing abuse or minimizing trauma.
- It is not reconciliation or giving the narcissist continued access to your life.

Forgiveness is an internal process, a conscious choice to release resentment, anger, and the emotional debt that keeps you tethered to the past.

It is a tool for your freedom, not a gift for the person who hurt you.

The Power of Acceptance

Acceptance does not mean approval of what happened.

It means:

- Acknowledging reality as it was.
- Recognizing that the abuse was never your fault.
- Understanding that you cannot change the past, only your relationship with it.

Acceptance allows you to:

- Stop fighting a battle that is already over.
- Redirect energy from anger and resentment toward healing and growth.
- Begin building a life unburdened by the past.

The Stages of Emotional Release

1. Acknowledgment
   - Admit the hurt and validate your feelings.
   - Example: *"I was mistreated, and it was not my fault."*
2. Processing Emotions
   - Use journaling, therapy, or creative outlets to express anger, grief, and sorrow.
   - These emotions are natural and necessary for healing.
3. Detachment
   - Recognize that the narcissist's actions do not define your worth.
   - Separate your identity and emotional health from their behavior.
4. Releasing Resentment
   - Gradually let go of the emotional hold the narcissist has over you.
   - Forgiveness and acceptance are personal acts, not obligations.

Setting the Stage for Forward Movement

To move forward, cultivate:

1. Self-Respect
   - o Maintain boundaries and honor your needs.
   - o Reaffirm that your well-being is a priority.
2. Self-Compassion
   - o Treat yourself with care as you process lingering pain.
3. Empowerment
   - o Recognize the resilience it took to survive your upbringing.
   - o Each conscious choice to heal strengthens your autonomy.
4. Hope and Vision
   - o Envision a life shaped by your values, not parental control.
   - o Set goals for emotional health, personal growth, and authentic relationships.

Tools to Facilitate Forgiveness and Acceptance

1. Journaling Letters (Unsent)

- Write to your parent without sending it.
- Express anger, sorrow, or disappointment.
- Conclude with statements like: *"I release you from my mind, and I reclaim my peace."*

2. Meditative Visualization

- Imagine placing your pain, resentment, or memories into a symbolic container.

- See it being released, leaving you lighter and freer.

3. Affirmations

- “I am no longer bound by what I endured.”
- “I deserve peace, love, and freedom from past pain.”
- Repeat daily to reinforce internal healing.

4. Therapeutic Support

- A therapist or support group can guide you through forgiveness and acceptance safely, without coercion or judgment.

Moving Forward Without the Narcissist’s Approval

Your healing and growth are not dependent on parental recognition or apology.

- Let go of the fantasy of their change or validation.
- Focus on yourself, your life, and your emotional autonomy.
- Reclaim time, energy, and emotional space for relationships, creativity, and joy.

Forward movement is a gradual, intentional process. Every step, no matter how small, is progress.

Now let’s take some time to reflect on the following questions. (Remember, take your time, be gentle with yourself)

1. What emotions are you ready to release today?
2. How can you forgive yourself for what you believed about yourself during childhood?
3. What aspects of your past do you need to accept without condoning them?

4. Which daily practices support emotional freedom and peace?
5. How does moving forward redefine your identity and life vision?

Forgiveness and acceptance are acts of self-liberation.

You are not forgiving the narcissist to restore them; you are forgiving to restore yourself.

You are not accepting the abuse to justify it; you are accepting reality to reclaim your power. Each act of release, each step toward peace, each assertion of self-worth moves you closer to the life you deserve: free, authentic, and unburdened by the shadows of the past.

Chapter 13:
Integration and the Path to Thriving

"Healing is not an endpoint — it is the art of living fully and authentically."

Bringing It All Together

By now, you've explored:

- The core wounds left by narcissistic parenting.
- How to set boundaries and assert your needs.
- Inner child work and self-compassion.
- Rebuilding self-esteem and identity.
- Cultivating healthy relationships.
- Practicing self-care and emotional regulation.
- Finding forgiveness and acceptance.

Integration means weaving these elements together into a coherent, empowered life.

It is the stage where survival transforms into thriving.

Redefining Thriving

Thriving is:

- Living according to your values, not others' expectations.
- Feeling safe, seen, and respected in relationships.
- Experiencing emotional resilience and flexibility.
- Enjoying self-expression, creativity, and autonomy.

- Moving forward without the weight of past conditioning.

It is not perfection. It is presence, growth, and authenticity.

Practical Steps for Integration

1. Daily Alignment with Your Values

- Reflect: Does this action, choice, or relationship align with my authentic self?
- Adjust where necessary to maintain congruence with who you truly are.

2. Consistent Self-Care and Emotional Check-Ins

- Make self-care non-negotiable.
- Monitor emotional triggers, boundaries, and inner child needs.

3. Boundary Reinforcement

- Continue practicing assertiveness in all areas of life.
- Respect yourself enough to maintain limits, even when challenged.

4. Celebrate Growth and Resilience

- Acknowledge the courage it took to survive, heal, and reclaim your life.
- Track milestones: saying no, reclaiming identity, nurturing healthy relationships.

5. Cultivate Joy and Purpose

- Engage in passions, creative pursuits, hobbies, and meaningful work.
- Surround yourself with people, places, and experiences that energize and inspire you.

Embracing Your Authentic Self

Integration is the culmination of reclaiming your true self.

- Authenticity: Speak, act, and live in alignment with your values.
- Resilience: Use past challenges as a foundation for strength.
- Empowerment: Make choices guided by self-respect and wisdom, not fear or obligation.
- Connection: Form relationships that honor mutual respect and emotional safety.

Your true self is not defined by childhood trauma — it is defined by your courage to heal, grow, and thrive.

Thriving in Practice

1. Mindful Living
    - Practice presence, gratitude, and intentionality in daily life.
2. Continued Inner Work
    - Healing is ongoing; revisit inner child work, boundary practices, and self-compassion regularly.
3. Personal Growth and Learning
    - Seek experiences that expand knowledge, skills, and self-awareness.
4. Contributing to Others
    - Healthy giving — mentoring, volunteering, or supporting others — fosters fulfillment without self-sacrifice.

Now let's take some time to reflect on the following questions. (Remember, take your time, be gentle with yourself)

1. What does thriving look like for you personally?
2. Which healing practices have been most transformative?
3. How can you maintain balance between self-care, relationships, and growth?
4. In what ways can you express authenticity daily?
5. What milestones can you celebrate as markers of thriving?

Thriving is not about erasing the past. It is about embracing your full story, honoring your resilience, and living intentionally. The adult child of a narcissistic parent is not destined to repeat patterns, to remain broken, or to live in fear. You are capable of love, joy, autonomy, and fulfillment. Healing is your choice, your journey, and your reclamation of life on your own terms. Step into your power, embrace your truth, and thrive.

There are a few books by different authors which has helped me a lot to see the truth spiritually and physically. I have listed them at the end of this book. These books have taught me to believe the truth and to rewire my mind. I am still studying, learning, and researching. I have listed them at the end of this book.

1. Kealy D, Ogrodniczuk JS. Pathological narcissism and the obstruction of love. Psychodyn Psychiatry. 2014 Mar;42(1):101-19. doi: 10.1521/pdps.2014.42.1.101. PMID: 24555464.
2. Weinberg I, Ronningstam E. Narcissistic Personality Disorder: Progress in Understanding and Treatment. Focus (Am Psychiatr Publ). 2022 Oct;20(4):368-377. doi: 10.1176/appi.focus.20220052. Epub 2022 Oct 25. PMID: 37200887; PMCID: PMC10187400.
3. **Why am I feeling "brain fog" and what exactly does that mean?**
4. **Boundaries Updated and Expanded Edition(Enlarged) : When to Say Yes, How to Say No To Take Control of Your Life : Henry Cloud, John Townsend: Amazon.in: Books**
5. The Confident Woman by Joyce Meyer
6. Making good habits and breaking bad habits by Joyce Meyer
7. Battlefield of the Mind by Joyce Meyer
8. Believe in yourself by Joseph murphy.
9. Emotional Intelligence by Daniel Goleman
10. The Let Them Theory by Mel Robbins